Spotlight on Scraps

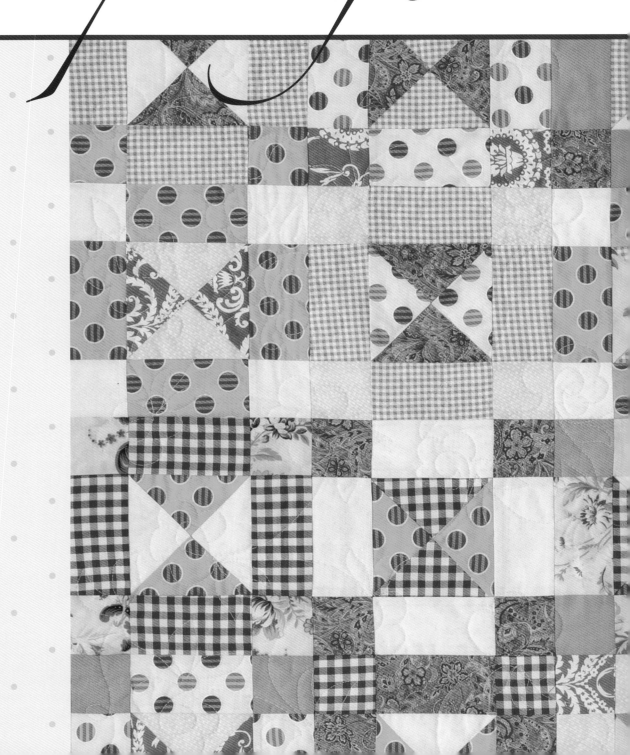

Spotlight on

Scraps

10 PRETTY QUILTS
CYNDI WALKER

Martingale®
& COMPANY

Spotlight on Scraps:
10 Pretty Quilts
Cyndi Walker
© 2008 by Cyndi Walker

That Patchwork Place® is an imprint
of Martingale & Company®.

Martingale & Company
20205 144th Ave. NE
Woodinville, WA 98072-8478 USA
www.martingale-pub.com

CREDITS

President & CEO: Tom Wierzbicki
Publisher: Jane Hamada
Editorial Director: Mary V. Green
Managing Editor: Tina Cook
Technical Editor: Darra Williamson
Copy Editor: Melissa Bryan
Design Director: Stan Green
Production Manager: Regina Girard
Illustrator: Adrienne Smitke
Cover Designer: Stan Green
Text Designer: Patricia Field
Photographer: Brent Kane

Printed in China
13 12 11 10 09 08   8 7 6 5 4 3 2 1

Library of Congress
Cataloging-in-Publication Data
Library of Congress Control Number:
2007045290

ISBN: 978-1-56477-779-9

contents

introduction

There is nothing quite like finding the fabric that happens be to the perfect shade of yellow for your current project, or a print that inspires you to start a whole new quilt. Through this book, I hope to share new ideas and the inspiration to dig through your scraps to rediscover the long-lost corners of your fabric stash.

Successful scrap quilts are full of life and energy that might never be found in the perfectly planned quilt. You can achieve spontaneity and excitement in your quilts by looking at what you already have on hand and then taking the steps toward fabric freedom. Even a quilt pattern that you may have made several times can take on new life with exciting new color and fabric choices. As you build your color confidence, you will start to see new possibilities in fabrics you might typically shy away from.

Unlock the joy of fabric freedom: put your quilts in the spotlight with scraps!

fabric know-how

All the projects in this book were made from high-quality, 100%-cotton fabrics. Typically, cotton is the fabric of choice for quilters. It is easy to use, gives crisp results when pressed, and is available in a wide assortment of colors. Using the best fabrics will ensure that your quilt lasts through many years of use and enjoyment.

To Prewash . . . or Not to Prewash?

Most quilters have an opinion—and an immediate answer—to the question of whether to prewash fabrics before using them in a quilt, and each will stand his or her ground firmly on the subject. If you are still uncertain, knowing the pros and cons of each option can help you make this decision.

Prewashing your fabric removes any sizing and residual dyes, and allows the fabric to shrink before you sew it into your quilt. Quilts that will see heavy use and repeated washings are good candidates for prewashed fabric, even if you typically don't take this preparatory step. Dark fabrics tend to bleed when washed, so it's best to have

this happen *before* you incorporate them into your quilt rather than running the risk of a dark print bleeding onto a lovely adjacent cream fabric.

On the other hand, many quilts are made for artistic purposes rather than daily use. For the makers of these quilts, prewashing is less of an issue as the quilts will most likely never be washed, or are so heavily embellished that washing them isn't even an option. There are also those on the "I don't prewash" side who *want* the fabrics to shrink slightly when washed to give the finished quilt a puckered, antique look.

Print Selection

The scale of the print on fabric, and how these printed fabrics are placed, plays a big part in the finished look of your quilt. Your choice of small "ditzy" prints, large dramatic prints, and everything in between gives you a wide range of opportunities to integrate scraps into your designs. Make the most of the fabric-selection process and embrace your basket of scraps.

Large-scale prints are a fun way to add variety to your quilt, and if cut and placed carefully, they can create the illusion of more than a single fabric. Prints with motifs that seemed too large or difficult to use suddenly take on a new life. For example, a colorful, large-scale floral print can yield some very interesting results when cut up into small squares—each square will have its own "personality" and can be worked into your quilt to add variety and visual excitement.

Prewash for Fusing

Chemicals used in the textile-manfacturing process can cause appliqué pieces to fuse poorly. If you have trouble with fusible web not adhering properly to your appliqué fabric, prewash your fabric. Omit any fabric softeners.

Large-scale fabrics are valuable additions to a scrap quilter's bag of tricks.

Subtle tone-on-tone prints give the eye a place to rest in a busy scrap quilt.

Not to be forgotten, tiny prints add fun and texture to your quilt. Small-scale prints juxtaposed with large- and medium-scale prints can create interesting contrasts. For your next project, try auditioning a wide variety of prints before making your final decisions. If you are the proud owner of a beloved scrap pile, dive in and see what you already have on hand before heading off to your favorite quilt shop.

Tone-on-tone or "tonal" fabrics can be a scrap quilter's best friend—well, heck, *any* quilter's best friend. These subtle prints add a sense of calm—a visual oasis—amid a sea of more active prints. When I shop for fabric, I often purchase tonal fabrics in my favorite colors or textures when I see them. These versatile fabrics have served me well when visual "chaos" threatened to overrun a work in progress.

The greater the range of prints you have, the richer your scrap quilt will be.

Why use just one fabric when you can use a variety of prints in a single color?

Building a Successful Palette

Many quilters struggle with color. Some actually dread choosing fabrics—enough so that many quilt shops have staff members who will gladly help out in a color-choice pickle.

To conquer the fear of color, start by working with colors you are comfortable with, and then slowly build up to more adventurous color combinations.

Broaden your horizons: If you have chosen the "perfect" yellow to use in your quilt, try substituting four *different* yellow prints in the same shade. Suddenly you have gone from using a single fabric to adding four new prints to your quilt. If you are feeling particularly brave, you can even try varying the value of these four new fabrics slightly— perhaps taking one a shade lighter and one a shade darker. Be a fabric rebel! This approach can work with any color and is often the way I delve into my projects.

If you are a saver of scraps, this is a great time to dig deep into your stash. Since quilters often revisit favorite color schemes, it's very likely that leftovers from past projects will work in your current quilt. That 4" square of fabric you couldn't seem to part with can find a happy home when you least expect it.

If you don't have a scrap pile to draw from, check with your local quilt shop: you may find "instant" scrap bags for sale, stuffed with odd cuts, remnants, and left-over pieces from the bolts on the shelves.

With each quilt you make, you will naturally accumulate scraps without trying. Quilting can be a messy business—you might as well recycle the leftovers!

Color Inspiration

Every project has a beginning, and that beginning often comes in the form of a piece of beautiful, inspirational fabric. For example, the colors in a gorgeous floral print can be the inspiration for building an entire color palette, even if—ironically—that original inspiration piece is scrapped from your final fabric selection. If the color combinations in the inspiration fabric speak to you, the color palette is probably a good candidate for your next project.

Multicolored fabrics often find their way into my quilts as "blender fabrics." A blender fabric is one that allows me to create harmony between colors that might not otherwise go together. Imagine, for example, that you have fallen in love with a selection of pink and green fabrics at your quilt shop. The fabrics look OK together, but will they make a good quilt? If you have to ask your-self that question, the answer is usually "not quite." Here is where the blenders work their magic. Find a beautiful fabric with both pink *and* green in the print, and see how it works

Blender fabrics help two or more diverse colors mix more successfully in your quilt.

with the various pink and green prints. Suddenly, one piece of fabric can make two other pieces of fabric "play nicely" together.

quilting basics

The following pages include information about the basic tools and techniques you'll need to make the quilts in this book. Read through the section now, and refer back to it as needed as you work on your project.

Supplies

A sewing room stocked with the following basic supplies ensures that you'll be ready to jump right in every time you sit down to stitch.

SEWING MACHINE. A sewing machine in good working order, with a reliable, even straight stitch, is key to any quilting project. A few "bells and whistles," such as a blanket or zigzag stitch for machine appliqué and the ability to lower your feed dogs for free-motion quilting, are nice features that will only add to your quilting experience.

ACRYLIC RULERS. Generally, the size ruler you'll need will depend on the size of your project. For the projects in this book, a 6½" x 12" ruler is very handy for general cutting, while an 8½" x 24" ruler is perfect for cutting borders and squaring your quilt. As you continue to make quilts, you may find other sizes helpful for making your tasks go more smoothly. Whatever size ruler you choose, be sure the grid lines are easily visible when you place the ruler on your fabric.

ROTARY CUTTER AND MAT. A rotary cutter with a sharp blade and a mat designed for cutting are must-haves for today's quilter. The cutting mat should be big enough to accommodate larger pieces of fabric comfortably. If you encounter issues with your blade not cutting through all layers of your fabric, replace the blade—it is probably nicked or dull.

PINS AND NEEDLES. Sharp, extra-fine silk pins with glass heads are the best choice for holding fabric pieces in place as you sew. Because they are sharp and thin, they glide through the fabric and reduce the shifting of matched points.

Keep a variety of needles—including basting needles—on hand for all types of sewing. For general machine piecing, an 80/12 Sharp needle is a good choice. For hand appliqué, a 10 or 11 Sharp works well.

THREAD. Cotton thread in a neutral color is a good choice for piecing. If you are working with dark fabric, you may want to consider a darker thread to avoid having any stitches show through when the seams are pressed. You can use a wide range of thread fibers and colors for machine appliqué and quilting, depending upon the look you wish to achieve. Rayon thread provides a nice sheen, while cotton thread has a clean, crisp finish. Experiment with both on a test piece of fabric to determine which you would like to use for each project. When working with hand-appliqué techniques, 50-weight or 60-weight cotton thread works well. Coordinate the color with your appliqué piece rather than with the background fabric.

SCISSORS. A sharp pair of scissors is a must for cutting fabric and appliqué pieces. Also consider a smaller pair of embroidery scissors for snipping threads and cutting curves. Using sewing scissors to cut paper dulls them quickly, so it is a good idea to have a pair of scissors reserved for paper.

SEAM RIPPER. As much as we hate to admit it, we all need a seam ripper from time to time to assist in removing stitches from pieces sewn together incorrectly.

MARKING TOOLS. For marking quilting patterns on a finished quilt top, I find that chalk works best. Water-soluble markers or quilter's pencils are also helpful tools for marking fabric. A mechanical pencil with a soft lead comes in handy for tracing templates onto fabric.

Whatever markers you plan to use, test them first on a scrap of fabric to be sure they are easy to see and—if necessary—easy to remove.

Rotary Cutting

Quilting has been changed enormously by the advent of the rotary cutter, which allows you to quickly and precisely cut fabric into strips, squares, and triangles.

Begin by pressing your fabric and then folding it in half, selvage to selvage. (If you are working with a large piece of fabric, you may wish to fold the fabric in half once again by bringing the folded edge to meet the selvage.) Place the folded edges of the fabric along a horizontal line on your cutting mat. Align your ruler with the left edge of the fabric, along a vertical line. Use your rotary cutter to trim and straighten the edge of the fabric, making sure that you are cutting through all of the fabric's layers.

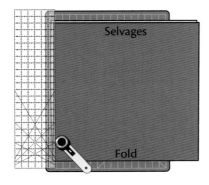

Many projects in this book instruct you to cut a strip of fabric and then crosscut this strip into smaller units such as squares and rectangles. To do this, cut the strip to the length and width indicated in the instructions, and then align the long cut edge of the strip with a horizontal line on your cutting mat. Use your ruler to trim the short edge of the strip even, measure the correct size of the piece you need, and cut the strip into smaller segments.

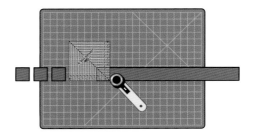

To cut half-square triangles from squares, align your ruler diagonally over the square from corner to corner and cut the square into two equally sized triangles. If the directions call for quarter-square triangles, carefully align the ruler diagonally in the opposite direction and make a second cut.

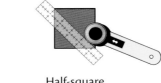

Half-square triangle

Quarter-square triangle

Machine Piecing

The success of any quilting project relies on the precision of a consistent ¼" seam. If your sewing machine has a ¼"-wide foot, you will find it easier to maintain accuracy. If your machine is not equipped with this attachment, you may be able to set the position of the needle to accommodate this width. You may also create a ¼" seam guide by measuring and then placing a piece of tape ¼" to the right of the needle as shown.

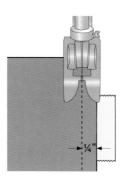

If you find that your finished units and blocks are not aligning correctly or are not quite measuring up, it may be that the ¼" seam is slightly off. Seam variances, even as little as ¹/₁₆", will multiply as you go along. This is especially true for smaller pieces and more complicated blocks. If you are unsure about the setting on your machine, try sewing along the edge of a scrap of fabric and then measuring the distance between the stitch line and the raw edge of the fabric. Adjust as necessary to achieve the perfect ¼" seam.

CHAIN PIECING

When you are faced with making large numbers of identical units, chain piecing can provide an efficient means of reaching your goal. Chain piecing is based on the assembly-line principle. Instead of stopping and clipping the thread between each unit, continue to stitch identical pieces in a chain-linked fashion, stopping to cut them apart only when you have reached the correct number of like units. This allows you to continue sewing without interruption.

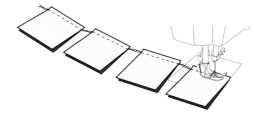

STRIP PIECING

You can make quick work of certain patchwork units and blocks by utilizing strip sets. This technique consists of sewing two or more strips of fabric together along their long edges and then crosscutting the strip sets into units or segments.

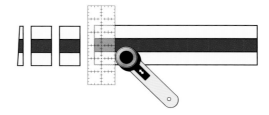

WORKING WITH TRIANGLES

Triangles have a reputation among quilters as being difficult to work with due to the stretch-prone bias edge created when the fabric is cut on a 45° angle. Once mastered, however, triangles can open doors to new and exciting quilts.

To minimize the distortion, handle triangles with care as you piece and press them. Many stray triangle points are caused by a last-minute flip in the direction of the seam allowance when the seam is sewn. To avoid this, use the tip of your seam ripper to hold the seam allowance in place as you sew. With a little practice, you will be on your way to perfect points and crisp pinwheels.

PRESSING

Mastering the art of pressing can make all the difference in achieving accuracy in patchwork. The key is to remember that pressing is *not* the same as ironing. Resist the urge to drag the iron back and forth; instead, lift and set it down while applying downward pressure. This method can help prevent distortion of the fabric, especially when you are working with the bias edges of triangles. The addition of steam during this process is also helpful for ensuring a crisply pressed block.

The general rule of thumb is to press seams toward the darkest fabric to avoid any dark colors showing through on the lighter fabrics. Instructions and diagrams for each project include pressing guidelines to assist you.

Machine Appliqué

Appliqué for the quilts in this book was done with fusible web and machine stitching, and the following instructions describe that method. The patterns accompanying the projects have been reversed for use with the fusible technique. If you prefer hand appliqué, reverse the patterns and add a ¼" turn-under allowance when cutting out the fabric shapes.

Before you begin, read the instructions for your chosen brand of fusible web to determine the recommended heat settings and fusing times.

1. Trace the appliqué patterns onto template plastic—available at many quilt and craft stores—and cut out each shape directly on the traced lines. Use an emery board to gently shape any rough edges of the plastic.

2. Use a mechanical pencil to trace the templates as directed onto the paper side of the fusible web. Avoid using ink to reduce any risk of transfer onto your fabric.

3. Cut the appliqué shapes out of the fusible web, leaving at least ¼" of web outside the pencil line. Also cut the fusible web from the center of each piece, ¼" inside the

pencil line; all that remains is ¼" of the fusible web on each side of the line. This helps keep your appliqué pieces soft to the touch when the stitching is finished.

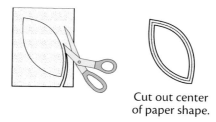

Cut out center
of paper shape.

4. Follow the manufacturer's instructions for the fusible web to adhere each shape onto the wrong side of the desired appliqué fabric. Remember: *press*, don't iron!

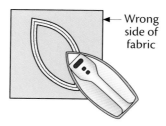

← Wrong side of fabric

5. Allow all fabric pieces to cool to room temperature after fusing. Carefully cut out each appliqué piece directly on the traced lines—this is the final, finished shape of your appliqué, so take care as you cut. Remove the paper backing from each piece.

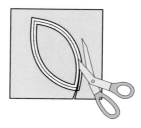

Easy Removal

If you find it difficult to remove the paper backing from the fusible web after it has been fused to fabric, try using a pin or a pair of tweezers to get started.

6. Press the fabric you have chosen as the background for your appliqué. Working at your ironing board, and referring to the appliqué placement diagram that accompanies the project, position each appliqué piece in place. Always begin with the appliqué shapes that will be overlapped by other shapes, or from "back to front." The patterns have been labeled alphabetically to help you with placement order. Fuse the appliqués in place.

7. Finish the outside (raw) edges of the appliqués using a machine blanket (buttonhole), zigzag, or other favorite decorative stitch. You can use either coordinating or contrasting thread depending on the look you prefer.

Working with Wool-Felt Appliqué

Wool-felt appliqué is very straightforward and can be a fast and easy way to add texture to your quilt top. Use a pencil to trace the appliqué template onto the dull side of freezer paper, and roughly cut the shape outside the traced line. Press the freezer paper waxy side down onto the wool, cut out the shape directly on the traced line, and remove the freezer paper. With a small amount of water-soluble glue, tack the shape in place onto the background fabric, and secure using a blanket stitch, French knots, or other decorative embroidery stitches.

Test First!

The dyes in wool felt—especially hand-dyed fabrics—have a tendency to bleed when wet. Test your wool felt for color-fastness prior to using it in your quilt.

Hand-Embroidery Stitches

Several of the projects in this book feature hand-embroidery stitches as embellishment. The illustrations below demonstrate the stitches used in these projects.

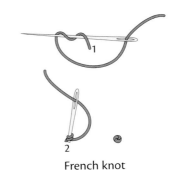

French knot

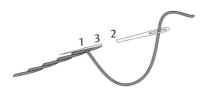

Stem stitch

Borders

When you have finished assembling the center area of your quilt, it is time to add the borders. The instructions for each project give you the appropriate cutting instructions for single-fabric borders, but it is always a good idea to measure your quilt before you cut the borders to ensure the best possible fit. This involves taking a measurement in three places: along the right (or top) edge, through the center, and along the left (or bottom) edge.

1. Measure the length of the quilt top through the center and along the two parallel outside edges. If the three measurements do not match, figure the average, and then cut the side border strips to this measurement. Find and mark the midpoints of the border strips and the side edges of the quilt.

Place the border strips right sides together with the sides of the quilt, matching the ends and midpoints, and pin in place. Sew and press as instructed, usually toward the border strips.

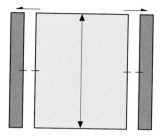

2. Measure the width of the quilt top through the center, including the side borders you just added; measure the two parallel outside edges as well. Average the measurements if necessary, and then cut the top and bottom border strips to this measurement. Find and mark the midpoints of the border strips and the top and bottom edges of the quilt. Place the border strips right sides together with the top and bottom of the quilt, matching the ends and midpoints; pin, sew, and press.

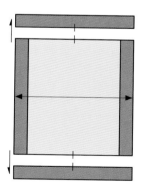

Finishing Techniques

You've put so much care into choosing the fabrics and assembling your quilt top, you'll want to make sure your quilting and binding techniques don't let you down. Here are some techniques to help you achieve a "perfect finish!"

ASSEMBLING THE LAYERS

Cut the quilt backing to measure 10" larger than the quilt in both length and width to allow for any shrinking that might occur during the quilting process. Materials listed for each project include the appropriate amount of fabric to purchase for the backing. If the width of the quilt plus the excess is larger than 40", you will need to piece the backing.

1. Divide the required fabric crosswise into two or three pieces of equal length as directed in the project instructions. Remove the selvages and sew the pieces together using a ½" seam. Press the seams open.

2. Spread the backing, wrong side up, on a clean, flat surface. Secure the edges of the backing to the working surface with masking tape to keeping the backing fabric smooth.

3. Center the batting and quilt top, right side up, over the backing, smoothing each layer as you go to avoid any puckering during the quilting process.

4. For machine quilting, work from the center of the quilt out toward the edges, and use safety pins to pin the three layers together, spacing the pins approximately 6" apart. For hand quilting, use a light-colored thread and large basting stitches instead of safety pins to secure the layers.

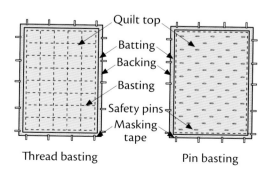

Thread basting   Pin basting

MACHINE QUILTING

The quilts in this book were quilted by machine, which is a great way to finish your projects quickly. For quilting straight lines, a walking foot is a handy tool that helps prevent puckering or shifting of the fabric layers as you quilt.

Walking foot

Some common straight-stitch designs include stitching in the ditch (stitching right along the seam line in key seams and around each shape) and outline quilting (stitching ¼" from the seam lines in each shape). These techniques are often used to highlight traditional designs or special piecing.

Quilting in the ditch   Outline quilting

For free-motion quilting, you need a machine with a darning foot and the capability to lower the feed dogs. With this technique, you don't turn the fabric under the needle, but instead guide the fabric in the direction of the design.

Darning foot

An easy way to get started with free-motion quilting is with a "stipple" or "meander" pattern. For quilts with appliqué, try stitching around the edges of the pieces to outline or highlight the shapes.

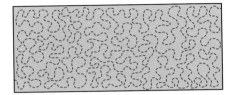

Free-motion quilting

Test for Success

It's always best to test your machine for tension and speed by using a small sandwich of batting and fabric from your current project.

For further guidance on machine-quilting techniques, look for *Machine Quilting Made Easy* by Maurine Noble (Martingale & Company, 1994).

BINDING

The projects in this book use the traditional French-fold method of binding. Each project lists adequate yardage for enough 2½" crosswise strips to cover the perimeter of the quilt, plus an additional 10" for seams, folding at the corners, and overlapping.

1. Cut the binding material across its width into the number of 2½" strips required for your project.

2. Piece the binding strips together end to end at right angles as shown to make a continuous strip. Trim any excess seam allowance to ¼" and press the seams open to reduce bulk. When you have sewn all the strips together, fold the strip in half lengthwise, wrong sides together, and press. Trim one end at a 45° angle, fold the trimmed end under, and press along the fold.

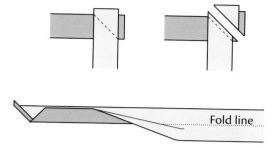

Fold line

3. Trim the batting and backing even with the quilt top. Start on one side of the quilt top with right sides together and raw edges aligned, and use a ¼"-wide seam to stitch the binding to the quilt. Begin a few inches from the start of the binding strip (this end will be used later to create a smooth end to the binding). Stop stitching ¼" from the first corner, backstitch, raise the needle, and clip the thread.

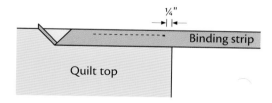

¼"

Binding strip

Quilt top

4. Rotate the quilt 90°. Fold the binding up, away from the quilt, and then back down onto itself, parallel with the edge of the quilt top. Resume sewing with a back-stitch at the edge of the quilt. This creates a sharp miter in the binding when you finish the corners in step 6.

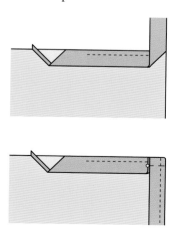

5. Continue sewing the binding to the edges of the quilt, turning the corners as described in step 4. Stop sewing when you are approximately 1" from the starting point of the binding. Overlap the starting point by 1" to 2", trim the excess binding at a 45° angle, and tuck the tail into the starting diagonal edge. Finish the binding seam.

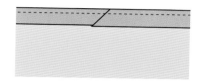

6. Fold the binding over the raw edges to the back of the quilt so that the edge of the binding covers the machine stitching. Use matching thread to blindstitch the folded edge of the binding in place and blindstitch the mitered corners.

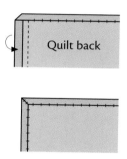

Quilt back

cherry cobbler

Fresh cherries are a favorite of mine and are twice as nice when worked into a quilt! Gingham ribbon, appliqué cherries, and a crisp color palette of red and white conjure images of picnics and lazy days in the park enjoying family and friends.

FINISHED QUILT: 62½" x 82½"
FINISHED BLOCK: 10" x 10"

Materials

Yardages are based on 42"-wide fabric.

- 3⅝ yards *total* of assorted white and cream prints for blocks
- 2⅛ yards *total* of assorted red prints for Pinwheel blocks, cherry appliqués, and inner border
- 1 yard of red print for outer border
- ⅓ yard *total* of assorted green prints for leaf appliqués
- ⅔ yard of fabric for binding
- 4 yards of fabric for backing (horizontal seam)
- 72" x 92" piece of batting
- 6 yards of ¼"-wide red-and-white gingham ribbon for cherry stems
- 1¼ yards of 18"-wide fusible web
- Water-soluble glue
- Thread in coordinating colors for appliqué
- Polyester monofilament thread

Cut the Fabric

Measurements include ¼" seam allowance. Cut all strips on the crosswise grain of the fabric (selvage to selvage).

From the assorted red prints, cut *a total of*:

- 36 squares, 3⅞" x 3⅞"; cut each square in half diagonally to make 72 half-square triangles
- 6 strips, 1½" x 42"
- 10 strips, 2½" x 42"
- 4 squares, 2½" x 2½"

From the assorted white and cream prints, cut *a total of*:

- 36 squares, 3⅞" x 3⅞"; cut each square in half diagonally to make 72 half-square triangles
- 6 strips, 1½" x 42"
- 72 rectangles, 2½" x 6½"
- 17 squares, 11½" x 11½"

From the red print for the outer border, cut:

- 7 strips, 4½" x 42"

From the binding fabric, cut:

- 8 strips, 2½" x 42"

From the gingham ribbon, cut:

- 51 pieces, ¼" x 4"

Make the Pinwheel Blocks

1. With right sides together, sew one red half-square triangle and one white or cream half-square triangle together along their diagonal edges as shown; press. Make 72 scrappy half-square-triangle units.

Make 72.

2. Arrange four half-square-triangle units from step 1 as shown. Sew the units in each row together; press. Sew the rows together; press. Make 18 scrappy pinwheel units.

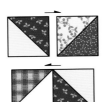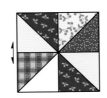

Make 18.

3. Sew one 1½"-wide red strip and one 1½"-wide white or cream strip together along their long edges to make a strip set as shown; press. Make six scrappy strip sets. Crosscut the strip sets into a total of 144 segments, 1½" wide. Arrange and sew two segments together as shown to make a four-patch unit; press. Make 72 scrappy four-patch units.

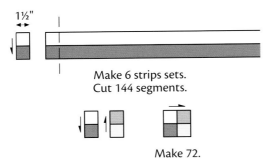

Make 6 strips sets.
Cut 144 segments.

Make 72.

4. Referring to the block assembly diagram below, arrange one unit from step 2, four units from step 3, and four 2½" x 6½"

white or cream rectangles as shown. Sew the units and rectangles together into rows; press. Sew the rows together to complete the block; press. Make 18 blocks. Each block should measure 10½" x 10½", including seam allowances.

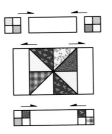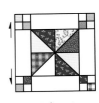

Make 18.

Make the Cherry Blocks

1. Referring to "Machine Appliqué" on pages 15, use the patterns on page 25 to prepare 51 cherry appliqués (A) using the assorted red prints and 17 regular and 17 reversed leaf appliqués (B) using the assorted green prints.

2. Referring to the appliqué placement diagram below, use a small amount of water-soluble glue to tack three ¼" x 4" gingham stem pieces in place on each 11½" white or cream square, trimming the stems as necessary. Position and fuse three cherry appliqués (A) and one regular and one reversed leaf appliqué (B) on each block, tucking the ends of the stems under the edges of the cherries and leaves; allow the appliqués to cool. Use coordinating thread to machine blanket stitch around the edges of each cherry and leaf. Use polyester monofilament thread to zigzag stitch the stems in place. Make 17 blocks.

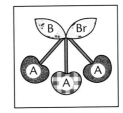

Appliqué placement
diagram

3. Trim each Cherry block to 10½" square.

Assemble the Quilt

1. Referring to the quilt assembly diagram below, arrange the Pinwheel and Cherry blocks in seven horizontal rows of five blocks each, alternating them as shown. Sew the blocks together into rows. Press the seams in opposite directions from row to row. Sew the rows together to complete the quilt center; press.

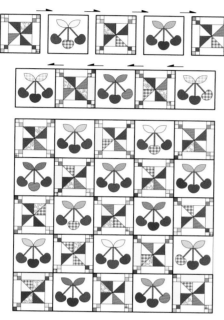

Assembly diagram

2. Arrange and sew five 2½"-wide assorted red strips together along their long edges to make a strip set as shown; press. Make two strip sets. Crosscut the strip sets into a total of 24 segments, 2½" wide.

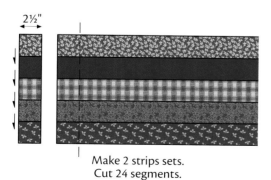

2½"

Make 2 strips sets.
Cut 24 segments.

3. Sew seven segments from step 2 together end to end to make one side inner-border strip as shown; press. Make two and sew them to the sides of the quilt. Press the seams toward the border.

Make 2.

4. Sew two 2½" red squares and five segments from step 2 together to make a top inner-border strip as shown; press. Repeat to make a bottom inner-border strip.

Make 2.

5. Sew the top and bottom inner-border strips from step 4 to the top and bottom of the quilt; press.

6. Sew the 4½"-wide red strips end to end to make one continuous strip; press. From this strip, cut two 4½" x 74½" outer-border strips, and sew them to the sides of the quilt. Press the seams toward the outer border.

7. From the remaining strip, cut two 4½" x 62½" outer-border strips, and sew them to the top and bottom of the quilt; press.

Finish the Quilt

For detailed instructions on the following steps, refer to "Finishing Techniques" on page 17.

1. Cut and piece the backing fabric so that it measures 10" larger than both the length and width of the quilt top.

2. Layer the quilt top, batting, and backing together; baste.

3. Machine or hand quilt as desired.

4. Use the 2½"-wide strips to prepare the binding, and sew the binding to the quilt.

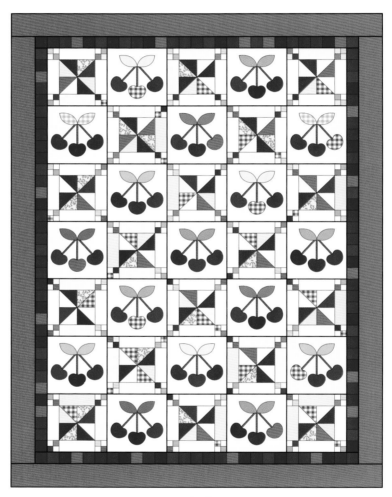

Quilt plan

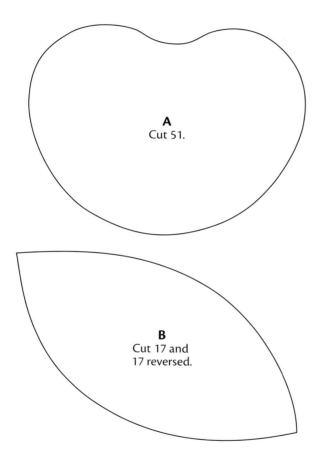

Patterns do not include
seam allowances.

A
Cut 51.

B
Cut 17 and
17 reversed.

strawberry lemonade

Intense, sun-drenched colors remind me of cool glasses of lemonade and hot summer days spent at the beach. A mix of bright yellow, hot coral red, and cool aqua prints perfectly captures the mood of those warm, wonderful days.

FINISHED QUILT: 60½" x 60½"
FINISHED BLOCK: 12" x 12"

Materials

Yardages are based on 42"-wide fabric.

- 2⅞ yards *total* of assorted yellow prints for blocks
- 1⅛ yards *total* of assorted coral red prints for blocks
- ⅝ yard *total* of assorted yellowish green prints for Log Cabin and Sixteen Patch blocks
- ½ yard *total* of assorted bluish green prints for Sixteen Patch and Sawtooth Star blocks
- ⅓ yard *total* of assorted white-on-white prints for Log Cabin and Sawtooth Star blocks
- ⅝ yard of fabric for binding
- 4 yards of fabric for backing
- 70" x 70" piece of batting

Cut the Fabric

Measurements include ¼" seam allowance. Cut all strips on the crosswise grain of the fabric (selvage to selvage).

From the assorted coral red prints, cut *a total of*:

- 8 squares, 2½" x 2½"
- 16 squares, 6⅞" x 6⅞"; cut each square in half diagonally to make 32 half-square triangles
- 40 squares, 2" x 2"

From the assorted white-on-white prints, cut *a total of*:

- 8 squares, 2½" x 2½"
- 40 squares, 2" x 2"

From the assorted yellow prints, cut *a total of*:

- 4 rectangles, 2½" x 4½"
- 4 rectangles, 2½" x 6½"
- 4 rectangles, 2½" x 8½"
- 4 rectangles, 2½" x 10½"
- 208 squares, 2⅝" x 2⅝"
- 16 squares, 6⅞" x 6⅞"; cut each square in half diagonally to make 32 half-square triangles
- 5 squares, 7¼" x 7¼"; cut each square in half twice diagonally to make 20 quarter-square triangles
- 20 squares, 3½" x 3½", in matching sets of 4

From the assorted yellowish green prints, cut *a total of*:

- 4 rectangles, 2½" x 6½"
- 4 rectangles, 2½" x 8½"
- 4 rectangles, 2½" x 10½"
- 4 rectangles, 2½" x 12½"
- 24 squares, 2⅝" x 2⅝"

From the assorted bluish green prints, cut *a total of*:

- 24 squares, 2⅝" x 2⅝"
- 20 squares, 3⅞" x 3⅞", in matching sets of 4; cut each square in half diagonally to make 40 half-square triangles

From the binding fabric, cut:

- 7 strips, 2½" x 42"

Make the Log Cabin Blocks

1. Arrange two 2½" coral red squares and two 2½" white squares as shown. Sew the squares together into rows; press. Sew the rows together, carefully matching the center seams; press. Make four four-patch units.

Make 4.

2. Sew a 2½" x 4½" yellow rectangle to the bottom edge of each unit from step 1 as shown; press. Sew a 2½" x 6½" yellow rectangle to the right edge of each unit; press. Make four.

3. Sew a 2½" x 6½" yellowish green rectangle to the top edge and a 2½" x 8½" yellowish green rectangle to the left edge of each unit from step 2 as shown; press. Make four.

4. Sew a 2½" x 8½" yellow rectangle to the bottom edge and a 2½" x 10½" yellow rectangle to the right edge of each unit from step 3 as shown; press. Make four.

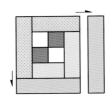

5. Sew a 2½" x 10½" yellowish green rectangle to the top edge and a 2½" x 12½" yellowish green rectangle to the left edge of each unit from step 4 as shown to complete the block; press. Make four blocks. Each block should measure 12½" x 12½", including seam allowances.

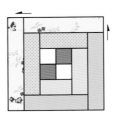

Make 4.

Make the Sixteen Patch Blocks

1. Arrange sixteen 2⅝" assorted yellow squares in four rows of four squares each as shown. Sew the squares together into rows; press. Sew the rows together; press. Make four sixteen-patch units.

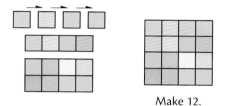

Make 4.

2. Repeat step 1, substituting two 2⅝" bluish green squares and two 2⅝" yellowish green squares for four of the 2⅝" yellow squares as shown. Make 12 sixteen-patch units.

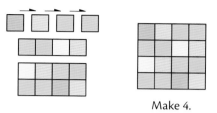

Make 12.

3. Fold a coral red half-square triangle in half along the long diagonal edge to find the center point; gently finger-press to make a crease. Match the crease to the center of one edge of a sixteen-patch unit from step 1 as shown; pin, stitch, and press. Sew coral red half-square triangles to the remaining sides of the unit to complete the block; press. Make four blocks and label them Sixteen

Patch block 1. Each block should measure 12½" x 12½", including seam allowances.

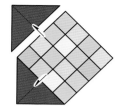 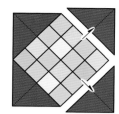

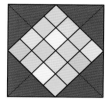

Block 1.
Make 4.

4. Repeat step 3, substituting a sixteen-patch unit from step 2 and four yellow half-square triangles as shown; press. Make four blocks and label them Sixteen Patch block 2. Each block should measure 12½" x 12½", including seam allowances.

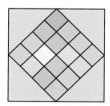

Block 2.
Make 4.

5. Repeat step 4, substituting two coral red half-square triangles for two yellow half-square triangles as shown; press. Make eight blocks and label them Sixteen Patch block 3. Each block should measure 12½" x 12½", including seam allowances.

Block 3.
Make 8.

Make the Sawtooth Star Blocks

1. With right sides together, sew a bluish green half-square triangle to the short edge of a yellow quarter-square triangle as shown; press. Sew a matching bluish green half-square triangle to the adjacent short edge of the yellow triangle to complete a flying-geese unit. Make 20 flying-geese units in matching sets of four.

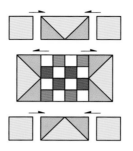

Make 20.

2. Arrange eight 2" coral red squares and eight 2" white squares in four rows of four squares each, alternating the squares as shown. Sew the squares together into rows; press. Sew the rows together; press. Make five sixteen-patch units.

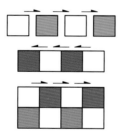

Make 5.

3. Referring to the block assembly diagram below, arrange four matching units from step 1, one unit from step 2, and four matching 3½" yellow squares as shown.

Sew the units and squares together into rows; press. Sew the rows together to complete the block; press. Make five blocks. Each block should measure 12½" x 12½" square, including seam allowances.

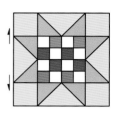

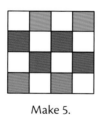

Make 5.

Assemble the Quilt

Referring to the quilt assembly diagram below, arrange the Log Cabin blocks, the Sixteen Patch blocks (1–3), and the Sawtooth Star blocks in five horizontal rows of five blocks each. Sew the blocks together into rows. Press the seam allowances in opposite directions from row to row. Sew the rows together to complete the quilt center; press.

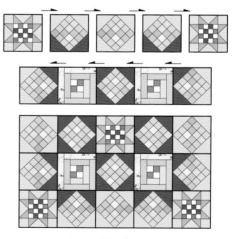

Assembly diagram

Finish the Quilt

For detailed instructions on the following steps, refer to "Finishing Techniques" on page 17.

1. Cut and piece the backing fabric so that it measures 10" larger than both the length and width of the quilt top.

2. Layer the quilt top, batting, and backing together; baste.

3. Machine or hand quilt as desired.

4. Use the 2½"-wide strips to prepare the binding, and sew the binding to the quilt.

Quilt plan

hopscotch

Shiny red buttons teamed with rich chocolate brown, warm yellow, and luscious cream prints make for a great game of quilting hopscotch. Dig into your button jar and baskets of scraps to make the most of this clever quilt.

Finished Quilt: 48½" x 48½"
Finished Block: 8" x 8"

Materials

Yardages are based on 42"-wide fabric.

- 1⅞ yards *total* of assorted brown prints for blocks and outer border
- 1¼ yards *total* of assorted cream 1 prints for blocks
- ⅔ yard of cream 2 print for inner and outer borders
- ¼ yard *total* of assorted yellow prints for blocks
- ½ yard of fabric for binding
- 3½ yards of fabric for backing
- 58" x 58" piece of batting
- 12 red buttons (½" to ⁹⁄₁₆" diameter)

Cut the Fabric

Measurements include ¼" seam allowance. Cut all strips on the crosswise grain of the fabric (selvage to selvage).

From the assorted brown prints, cut *a total of*:

- 104 squares, 2½" x 2½"
- 1 strip, 2½" x 42"
- 2 strips, 1½" x 42"
- 24 rectangles, 2½" x 8½", in matching pairs*

- 24 rectangles, 2½" x 4½", in matching pairs*
- 10 squares, 5¼" x 5¼"; cut each square in half twice diagonally to make 40 quarter-square triangles
- 2 squares, 4⅞" x 4⅞"; cut each square in half diagonally to make 4 half-square triangles

From the assorted cream 1 prints, cut *a total of*:

- 52 squares, 4½" x 4½"
- 48 squares, 2½" x 2½"

From the assorted yellow prints, cut *a total of*:

- 2 strips, 1½" x 42"
- 1 strip, 2½" x 42"

From the cream 2 print, cut:

- 5 strips, 2½" x 42"
- 11 squares, 5¼" x 5¼"; cut each square in half twice diagonally to make 44 quarter-square triangles

From the binding fabric, cut:

- 6 strips, 2½" x 42"

    Cut these in matching sets of two 2½" x 8½" rectangles and two 2½" x 4½" rectangles.

HOPSCOTCH

Make the Cross Blocks

1. Use a ruler and your preferred marker to mark a light diagonal line on the wrong side of each 2½" brown square. With right sides together, align a marked square with opposite corners of a 4½" cream 1 square as shown. Stitch directly on the marked lines and trim, leaving a ¼" seam allowance; press. Make 52 scrappy units.

Make 52.

2. Referring to the block assembly diagram below, arrange four units from step 1 as shown. Sew the units together into rows; press. Sew the rows together to complete the block; press. Make 13 blocks. Each block should measure 8½" x 8½", including seam allowances.

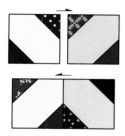 

Make 13.

Make the Snowball Blocks

1. Sew the two 1½"-wide yellow strips and the 2½"-wide brown strip together along their long edges, alternating them as shown to make strip set A; press. Crosscut the strip set into 24 segments, 1½" wide.

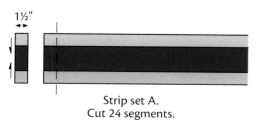

Strip set A.
Cut 24 segments.

2. Sew the two 1½"-wide brown strips and the 2½" yellow strip together along their long edges, alternating them as shown to make strip set B; press. Crosscut the strip set into 12 segments, 2½" wide.

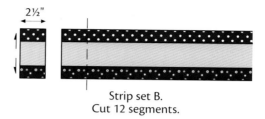

Strip set B.
Cut 12 segments.

3. Arrange two segments from step 1 and one segment from step 2 as shown. Sew the segments together; press. Make 12 scrappy units.

Make 12.

4. Use a ruler and your preferred marker to mark a light diagonal line on the wrong side of each 2½" cream 1 square. With right sides together, align a marked square with opposite ends of a 2½" x 8½" brown rectangle as shown. Stitch directly on the marked lines and trim, leaving a ¼" seam allowance; press. Make 24 units in matching pairs.

Make 24.

5. Referring to the block assembly diagram below, arrange one unit from step 3, two matching units from step 4, and two matching 2½" x 4½" brown rectangles as shown. Sew the units and rectangles together into rows; press. Sew the rows together to complete the block; press. Make 12 blocks. Each block should measure 8½" x 8½", including seam allowances.

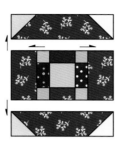 

Make 12.

Assemble the Quilt

1. Referring to the quilt assembly diagram below, arrange the Cross and Snowball blocks into five horizontal rows of five blocks each, alternating them as shown. Sew the blocks together into rows. Press the seams in opposite directions from row to row. Sew the rows together to complete the quilt center; press.

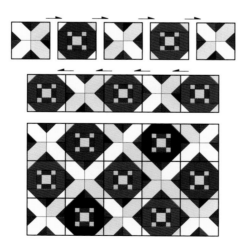

2. Sew the 2½"-wide cream 2 strips end to end to make one continuous strip; press. From this strip, cut two 2½" x 40½" inner-border strips, and sew them to the sides of the quilt. Press the seams toward the border.

3. From the remaining strip, cut two 2½" x 44½" inner-border strips, and sew them to the top and bottom of the quilt; press.

4. With right sides together, sew 10 assorted brown quarter-square triangles and 11 cream 2 quarter-square triangles together along their short edges, alternating them as shown; press. Make four outer-border strips.

Measure as You Go

Stop periodically to measure your pieced-triangle border to ensure it will finish to the correct length. The edge of the border that you sew to the quilt should measure 44½" long, including seam allowances.

5. Referring to the photo on page 32, sew an outer-border strip from step 4 to opposite sides of the quilt. Press the seams toward the outer border. Sew the remaining outer-border strips to the top and bottom of the quilt; press. Finish by sewing a brown half-square triangle to each corner of the quilt top. Press the seams toward the corner triangles.

Finish the Quilt

For detailed instructions on the following steps, refer to "Finishing Techniques" on page 17.

1. Cut and piece the backing fabric so that it measures 10" larger than both the length and width of the quilt top.

2. Layer the quilt top, batting, and backing together; baste.

3. Machine or hand quilt as desired.

4. Use the 2½"-wide strips to prepare the binding, and sew the binding to the quilt.

5. Referring to the quilt photo, sew a red button in the center of each Snowball block with matching thread.

Quilt plan

tickled pink

Pink, pink, and more pink! Have a great time combining bright and bold pinks with crisp white to create a sweet, playful confection that will fit right into the home of anyone who loves pink.

FINISHED QUILT: 44½" x 52½"
FINISHED BLOCK: 8" x 8"

Materials

Yardages are based on 42"-wide fabric.

- ⅝ yard of white-on-white print for inner border
- ½ yard *each* of 5 assorted light pink prints for blocks and outer border
- ½ yard *each* of 5 assorted medium pink prints for blocks and outer border
- ½ yard of fabric for binding
- 3 yards of fabric for backing (horizontal seam)
- 54" x 62" piece of batting

Cut the Fabric

Measurements include ¼" seam allowance. Cut all strips on the crosswise grain of the fabric (selvage to selvage).

From *each* of the 5 assorted light pink prints, cut:

- 2 squares, 5¼" x 5¼"; cut each square in half twice diagonally to make 8 quarter-square triangles (40 total)
- 3 strips, 2½" x 42"; crosscut into:
  - 16 rectangles, 2½" x 4½" (80 total)
  - 8 squares, 2½" x 2½" (40 total)

From *one* of the light pink prints, cut:

- 4 squares, 4½" x 4½"

From *each* of the 5 assorted medium pink prints, cut:

- 2 squares, 5¼" x 5¼"; cut each square in half twice diagonally to make 8 quarter-square triangles (40 total)
- 3 strips, 2½" x 42"; crosscut into:
  - 16 rectangles, 2½" x 4½" (80 total)
  - 8 squares, 2½" x 2½" (40 total)

From the white-on-white print, cut:

- 4 strips, 2½" x 42"

From the binding fabric, cut:

- 6 strips, 2½" x 42"

Make the Hourglass Blocks

1. Arrange two matching light pink quarter-square triangles and two matching medium pink quarter-square triangles as shown. With right sides together, sew a light and a medium triangle together along their short edges; press. Make two. Sew the units together; press. Make 20 hourglass units.

Make 20.

2. Referring to the block assembly diagram below, arrange a unit from step 1, four matching 2½" light pink squares, and four matching 2½" x 4½" medium pink rectangles as shown. Sew the unit, squares, and rectangles together into rows; press. Sew the rows together to complete the block; press. Make 10 blocks. Repeat, substituting four 2½" medium pink squares and four 2½" x 4½" light pink rectangles. Make 10. Each block should measure 8½" x 8½", including seam allowances.

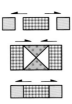

Make 10.   Make 10.

Assemble the Quilt

1. Referring to the quilt assembly diagram below, arrange the blocks into five horizontal rows of four blocks each as shown. Sew the blocks together into rows. Press the seams in opposite directions from row to row. Sew the rows together to complete the quilt center; press.

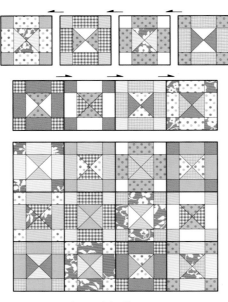

Assembly diagram

2. Sew the 2½"-wide white strips end to end to make one continuous strip; press. From this strip, cut two 2½" x 40½" inner-border strips, and sew them to the sides of the quilt. Press the seams toward the quilt center.

3. From the remaining strip, cut two 2½" x 36½" inner-border strips, and sew them to the top and bottom of the quilt; press.

4. Sew 22 of the remaining light and medium pink rectangles together along their long edges as shown; press. Make two outer-border strips and sew them to the sides of the quilt. Press the seams toward the outer border.

Make 2.

5. Sew 18 of the light and medium pink rectangles together along their long edges; press. Make two outer-border strips. Sew a 4½" light pink square to each end of each strip as shown; press. Make two and sew them to the top and bottom of the quilt; press.

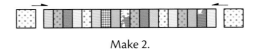

Make 2.

Finish the Quilt

For detailed instructions on the following steps, refer to "Finishing Techniques" on page 17.

1. Cut and piece the backing fabric so that it measures 10" larger than both the length and width of the quilt top.

2. Layer the quilt top, batting, and backing together; baste.

3. Machine or hand quilt as desired.

4. Use the 2 ½"-wide strips to prepare the binding, and sew the binding to the quilt.

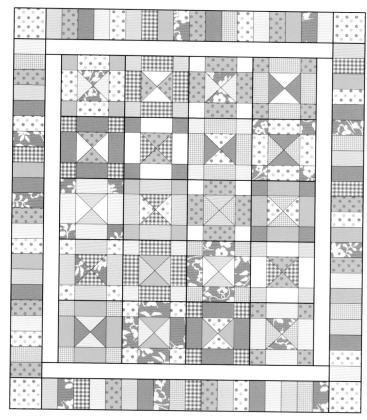

Quilt plan

lilac garden

Enchanting large-scale florals combine with polka dots and plaids to bring a springtime garden into your home. Don't be afraid to mix up your prints—the results can make for unexpected quilting fun!

FINISHED QUILT: 64½" x 98½"
FINISHED BLOCK: 12" x 12"

Materials

Yardages are based on 42"-wide fabric.

- 2⅝ yards *total* of assorted purple prints for blocks and outer border
- 2⅛ yards *total* of assorted cream floral prints for blocks and outer border
- 1⅝ yards of purple tone-on-tone floral print for setting triangles and inner border
- 1⅜ yards *total* of assorted yellow prints for blocks and outer border
- ¾ yard of fabric for binding
- 6 yards of fabric for backing (vertical seam)
- 74" x 108" piece of batting

Cut the Fabric

Measurements include ¼" seam allowance. Cut all strips on the crosswise grain of the fabric (selvage to selvage).

From the assorted cream floral prints, cut *a total of*:

- 15 rectangles, 2½" x 4½"
- 15 rectangles, 2½" x 8½"
- 32 squares, 4½" x 4½", in matching sets of 4
- 16 squares, 3⅜" x 3⅜"
- 8 squares, 5¼" x 5¼"; cut each square in half twice diagonally to make 32 quarter-square triangles

From the assorted purple prints, cut *a total of*:

- 15 squares, 4½" x 4½"
- 15 rectangles, 2½" x 6½"
- 15 rectangles, 2½" x 8½"
- 15 rectangles, 2½" x 10½"
- 15 rectangles, 2½" x 12½"
- 16 squares, 5¼" x 5¼", in matching pairs; cut each square in half twice diagonally to make 64 quarter-square triangles

From the assorted yellow prints, cut *a total of*:

- 15 rectangles, 2½" x 6½"
- 15 rectangles, 2½" x 10½"
- 16 squares, 3⅜" x 3⅜"

From the assorted purple, cream floral, and yellow prints, cut *a total of*:

- 308 squares, 2½" x 2½"

From the purple tone-on-tone floral print, cut:

- 8 strips, 3" x 42"
- 3 squares, 18¼" x 18¼"; cut each square in half twice diagonally to make 12 quarter-square triangles

- 2 squares, 9⅜" x 9⅜"; cut each square in half diagonally to make 4 half-square triangles

From the binding fabric, cut:

- 9 strips, 2½" x 42"

Make the Log Cabin Blocks

1. Sew a 2½" x 4½" cream rectangle to the bottom edge of a 4½" purple square as shown; press. Sew a 2½" x 6½" yellow rectangle to the right edge of the unit; press. Make 15.

Make 15.

2. Sew a 2½" x 6½" purple rectangle to the top edge and a 2½" x 8½" purple rectangle to the left edge of each unit from step 1 as shown; press. Make 15.

3. Sew a 2½" x 8½" cream rectangle to the bottom edge and a 2½" x 10½" yellow rectangle to the right edge of each unit from step 2 as shown; press. Make 15.

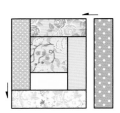

4. Sew a 2½" x 10½" purple rectangle to the top edge and a 2½" x 12½" purple rectangle to the left edge of each unit from step 3 as shown to complete the block; press. Make 15 blocks. Each block should measure 12½" x 12½", including seam allowances.

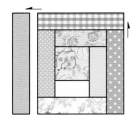

Make 15.

Make the Star Blocks

1. Arrange two 3⅜" yellow squares and two 3⅜" cream squares as shown. Sew the squares together into rows; press. Sew the rows together, carefully matching the center seam; press. Make eight four-patch units. Trim each unit to 6⅛" x 6⅛".

Make 8.

2. Sew a purple quarter-square triangle to one side of a 4½" cream square as shown; press. Sew a matching purple quarter-square triangle to the adjacent side of the square; press. Make 32 in matching sets of four.

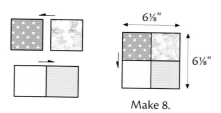

Make 32.

3. Sew a matching unit from step 2 to opposite sides of a unit from step 1 as shown; press. Make eight.

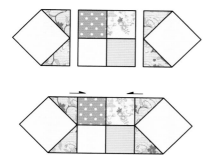

Make 8.

4. Sew a matching cream quarter-square triangle to opposite sides of each remaining unit from step 2 as shown; press. Make 16 in matching pairs.

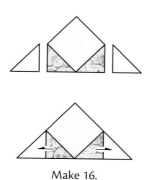

Make 16.

5. Referring to the block assembly diagram below, sew a matching unit from step 4 to the top and bottom of each unit from step 3 to complete the block; press. Make eight blocks. Each block should measure 12½" x 12½", including seam allowances.

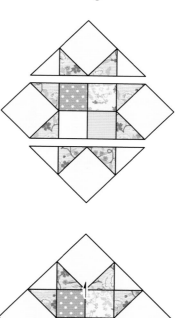

Make 8.

Assemble the Quilt

1. Referring to the quilt assembly diagram below, arrange the Log Cabin blocks, the Star blocks, the purple tone-on-tone quarter-square side setting triangles, and the purple tone-on-tone half-square corner setting triangles in diagonal rows as shown. Sew the blocks and side setting triangles together into rows; press. Sew the rows together; press. Complete the quilt center by adding the corner setting triangles. Press the seams toward the corner triangles.

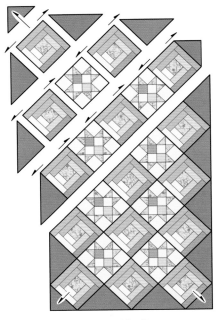

Assembly diagram

2. Sew the 3"-wide purple tone-on-tone strips end to end to make one continuous strip; press. From this strip, cut two 3" x 85½" inner-border strips, and sew them to the sides of the quilt. Press the seams toward the border.

3. From the remaining strip, cut two 3" x 56½" inner-border strips, and sew them to the top and bottom of the quilt; press.

Make and Add the Outer Border

The pieced outer-border strips are composed of purple, cream, and yellow squares randomly sewn into four-patch units and stitched together to capture the look of a true scrap quilt.

1. Referring to step 1 of "Make the Star Blocks" on page 45, make a total of 76 four-patch units using 2½" assorted purple, cream, and yellow squares. Sew 22 four-patch units and two additional 2½" assorted squares together to make a pieced outer-border strip as shown; press. Make two and sew them to the sides of the quilt. Press the seams toward the outer border.

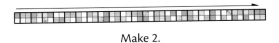

Make 2.

2. Sew 16 four-patch units from step 1 together to make an outer-border strip; press. Make two and sew them to the top and bottom of the quilt; press.

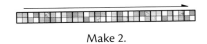

Make 2.

Finish the Quilt

For detailed instructions on the following steps, refer to "Finishing Techniques" on page 17.

1. Cut and piece the backing fabric so that it measures 10" larger than both the length and width of the quilt top.

2. Layer the quilt top, batting, and backing together; baste.

3. Machine or hand quilt as desired.

4. Use the 2½"-wide strips to prepare the binding, and sew the binding to the quilt.

Quilt plan

dutch tulips

The inspiration for this charming quilt comes from the beautifully hand-painted window boxes that adorn our home. With its tulips and floral accents, the quilt captures the look perfectly. Color and contrast are the keys to success; the striking black accents make the pinks and blues sing.

FINISHED QUILT: 52½" x 52½"
FINISHED TULIP BLOCK: 16" x 16"
FINISHED STAR BLOCK: 8" x 8"

Materials

Yardages are based on 42"-wide fabric.

- 1⅓ yards of black 1 tone-on-tone print for inner border, outer border, and Star blocks
- 1⅛ yards *total* of assorted light and medium blue prints for tulip stem and tulip petal appliqués, outer border, and Star blocks
- 1 yard *total* of assorted light and medium pink prints for tulip stem and tulip petal appliqués, outer border, and Star blocks
- ⅝ yard *total* of assorted black 2 tone-on-tone and other small-scale prints for outer border
- ¼ yard of yellow floral print for circle appliqués
- 2 squares, 9½" x 9½", of *each* of 2 medium green tone-on-tone prints for tulip stem appliqués
- 2 squares, 9½" x 9½", of *each* of 2 light pink tone-on-tone prints for appliqué backgrounds
- 2 squares, 9½" x 9½", of *each* of 2 medium pink tone-on-tone prints for appliqué backgrounds
- 2 squares, 9½" x 9½", of *each* of 2 light blue tone-on-tone prints for appliqué backgrounds
- 2 squares, 9½" x 9½", of *each* of 2 medium blue tone-on-tone prints for appliqué backgrounds
- ½ yard of fabric for binding
- 3½ yards of fabric for backing
- 62" x 62" piece of batting
- 2½ yards of 18"-wide fusible web
- Thread in coordinating colors for appliqué

Cut the Fabric

Measurements include ¼" seam allowance. Cut all strips on the crosswise grain of the fabric (selvage to selvage).

From the assorted light and medium blue prints, cut *a total of:*

- 16 squares (from the lighter prints), 2⅞" x 2⅞", in matching sets of four; cut each square in half once diagonally to make 32 half-square triangles
- 16 squares (from the darker prints), 2½" x 2½", in matching sets of four
- 8 strips (4 from the lighter prints and 4 from the darker prints), 2" x 15"

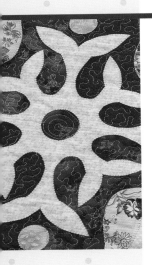

From the assorted light and medium pink prints, cut *a total of:*

- 4 squares (from the darker prints), 2½" x 2½"
- 4 squares (from the darker prints), 4½" x 4½"
- 8 strips (4 from the lighter prints and 4 from the darker prints), 2" x 15"

From the black 1 tone-on-tone print, cut:

- 4 squares, 5¼" x 5¼"; cut each square in half twice diagonally to make 16 quarter-square triangles

- 16 squares, 2½" x 2½"
- 4 strips, 2½" x 32½"
- 8 strips, 3" x 36½"

From the assorted black 2 tone-on-tone fabrics, cut *a total of:*

- 16 strips, 2" x 15"

From the binding fabric, cut:

- 6 strips, 2½" x 42"

Make the Tulip Blocks

1. Arrange the four 9½" light pink squares as shown. Sew the squares together into rows; press. Sew the rows together, carefully matching the center seams; press. Repeat using the 9½" medium pink squares, the 9½" light blue squares and the 9½" medium blue squares to make a total of four Four Patch blocks.

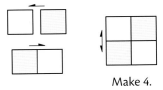

Make 4.

2. Referring to "Machine Appliqué" on page 15, use the patterns on page 55 to prepare four tulip stem appliqués (A) using the green and assorted light blue and light pink prints; 16 small tulip petal appliqués (B) using assorted light pink and light blue prints; 16 large tulip petal appliqués (C) using assorted medium pink and medium blue prints; and 16 tulip circle appliqués (D), four star circles (E), and four corner-square circles (F) using the yellow print. Set the star circles (E) and corner-square circles (F) aside for now.

3. Referring to the appliqué placement diagram below, position and fuse one tulip stem appliqué (A), four small and four large tulip petal appliqués (B and C), and four tulip circle appliqués (D) on each block from step 1; allow the appliqués to cool. Use coordinating thread to machine blanket stitch around the edges of each appliqué piece. Make four blocks.

4. Trim each Tulip block to 16½" square.

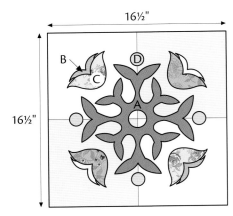

Appliqué placement diagram

Make the Star Blocks

1. With right sides together, sew a lighter blue half-square triangle to the short edge of a black 1 quarter-square triangle as shown; press. Sew a matching lighter blue half-square triangle to the adjacent short edge of the black triangle to complete a flying-geese unit. Make 16 flying-geese units in matching sets of four.

Make 16.

2. Use a ruler and your preferred marker to mark a light diagonal line on the wrong side of each 2½" darker blue square. With right sides together, align a marked square with opposite corners of a 4½" darker pink square as shown. Stitch directly on the marked line and trim, leaving a ¼" seam allowance; press. Repeat to sew matching 2½" blue squares to the remaining corners; press. Make four.

Make 4.

3. Position and fuse one star circle (E) in the center of each unit from step 2 as shown; allow the appliqués to cool. Use coordinating thread to machine blanket stitch around the edges of each appliqué piece. Make four.

Make 4.

4. Referring to the block assembly diagram below, arrange four matching flying-geese units from step 1, one unit from step 3, and four 2½" black 1 squares as shown. Sew the squares and units together into rows; press. Sew the rows together to complete the block; press. Make four blocks. Each block should measure 8½" x 8½", including seam allowances.

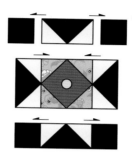 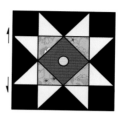

Make 4.

Assemble the Quilt

1. Referring to the quilt assembly diagram on page 53, arrange the Tulip blocks in two rows of two blocks each as shown. Sew the blocks together into rows; press. Sew the rows together. Press the center seam open.

2. Sew a 2½" x 32½" black 1 strip to opposite sides of the unit from step 1; press.

3. Position and fuse one corner-square circle (F) in the center of each 2½" darker pink square; allow the appliqués to cool. Use coordinating thread to machine blanket stitch around the edges of each appliqué piece. Make four.

Make 4.

4. Sew a unit from step 3 to each end of each remaining 2½" x 32½" black 1 strip as shown; press. Make two and sew them to the top and bottom of the quilt to complete the quilt center; press.

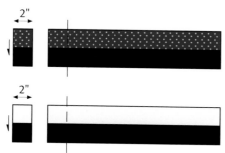

Make 2.

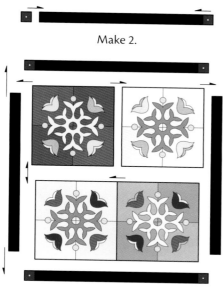

Assembly diagram

Make and Add the Outer Border

1. Sew one 2" x 15" black 2 strip and one darker pink 2" x 15" strip together along their long edges to make a strip set as shown; press. Then sew one 2" x 15" black 2 strip and one 2" x 15" lighter blue strip together in the same way. Make four strip sets in each color combination. Crosscut each strip set into six segments, 2" wide (48 segments total).

2"

2"

Make 4 strip sets in each color combination.
Cut 6 segments from each strip set.

2. Repeat step 1 to make eight more strip sets, substituting darker blue strips for the darker pink strips and substituting lighter pink strips for the lighter blue strips. Crosscut each strip set into six segments, 2" wide (48 segments total).

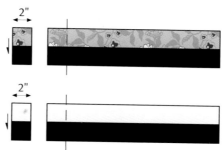

2"

2"

Make 4 strip sets in each color combination.
Cut 6 segments from each strip set.

3. Sew 24 segments from steps 1 and 2 together as shown; press. Make four.

Make 4.

If the pieced border units finish just a tiny bit short, try pressing them to length with a touch of spray starch.

4. Sew a 3" x 36½" black 1 strip to both long edges of each unit from step 3; press. Make four outer-border units. Each border unit should measure 8½" x 36½", including seam allowances.

Make 4.

5. Referring to the photo on page 48, sew an outer-border unit from step 4 to opposite sides of the quilt. Press the seams toward the outer border. Sew a Star block to each end of each remaining border unit as shown; press. Make two and sew them to the top and bottom of the quilt; press.

Make 2.

Finish the Quilt

For detailed instructions on the following steps, refer to "Finishing Techniques" on page 17.

1. Cut and piece the backing fabric so that it measures 10" larger than both the length and width of the quilt top.

2. Layer the quilt top, batting, and backing together; baste.

3. Machine or hand quilt as desired.

4. Use the 2½"-wide strips to prepare the binding, and sew the binding to the quilt.

Quilt plan

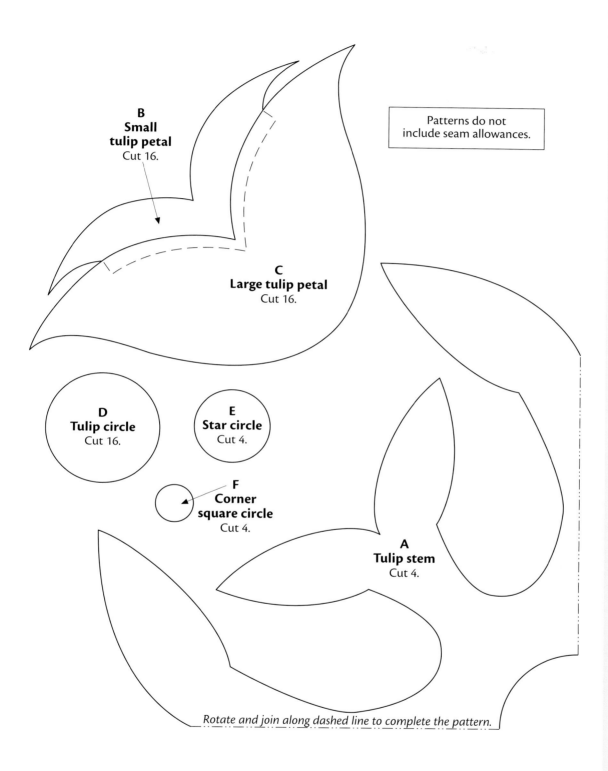

B
Small
tulip petal
Cut 16.

C
Large tulip petal
Cut 16.

Patterns do not
include seam allowances.

D
Tulip circle
Cut 16.

E
Star circle
Cut 4.

F
Corner
square circle
Cut 4.

A
Tulip stem
Cut 4.

Rotate and join along dashed line to complete the pattern.

autumn stars

Snuggle up under this cozy quilt—perfect for taking the chill off those clear, crisp, starry autumn nights. The warm colors and comforting tones of brown, red, and cream prints make for the perfect fireside combination.

FINISHED QUILT: 68½" x 86½"
FINISHED LARGE STAR BLOCK: 16" x 16"
FINISHED SMALL STAR BLOCK: 8" x 8"

Materials

Yardages are based on 42"-wide fabric.

- 2¼ yards *total* of assorted medium and dark brown prints for blocks
- 1¾ yards *total* of assorted red prints for blocks
- 1⅓ yards of tan 2 print for Small Star blocks and border
- 1 yard of cream 2 print for Small Star blocks and border
- ¾ yard *total* of assorted cream 1 and tan 1 prints for blocks and corner squares
- ¾ yard of dark brown print for sashing
- ⅓ yard *total* of assorted blue prints for blocks
- ¾ yard of fabric for binding
- 5⅓ yards of fabric for backing
- 78" x 96" piece of batting

Cut the Fabric

Measurements include ¼" seam allowance. Cut all strips on the crosswise grain of the fabric (selvage to selvage).

From the assorted medium and dark brown prints, cut *a total of*:

- 96 squares, 2½" x 2½"
- 24 squares, 5¼" x 5¼" in matching pairs; cut each square in half diagonally to make 48 half-square triangles
- 12 squares, 9¼" x 9¼"; cut each square in half twice diagonally to make 48 quarter-square triangles
- 28 rectangles, 1½" x 2½"
- 28 rectangles, 1½" x 4½"

From the assorted tan 1 and cream 1 prints, cut *a total of*:

- 126 squares, 2½" x 2½"
- 28 squares, 1½" x 1½"

From the assorted blue prints, cut *a total of*:

- 24 squares, 2½" x 2½"
- 28 squares, 1½" x 1½"

From the assorted red prints, cut *a total of*:

- 24 squares, 3¾" x 3¾", in matching sets of four; cut each square in half diagonally to make 48 half-square triangles
- 48 squares, 4⅞" x 4⅞", in matching sets of four; cut each square in half diagonally to make 96 half-square triangles
- 56 squares, 2⅞" x 2⅞"; cut each square in half diagonally to make 112 half-square triangles

From the dark brown print for sashing, cut:

- 9 strips, 2½" x 42"; crosscut into 17 strips, 2½" x 16½"

From the tan 2 print, cut:

- 1 strip, 5¼" x 42"; crosscut into 7 squares, 5¼" x 5¼". Cut each square in half twice diagonally to make 28 quarter-square triangles.
- 4 strips, 2½" x 42"; crosscut into 56 squares, 2½" x 2 ½"
- 10 strips, 2½" x 42"

From the cream 2 print, cut:

- 1 strip, 5¼" x 42"; crosscut into 7 squares, 5¼" x 5¼". Cut each square in half twice diagonally to make 28 quarter-square triangles.
- 5 strips, 4½" x 42"

From the binding fabric, cut:

- 9 strips, 2½" x 42"

Make the Large Star Blocks

1. Arrange two 2½" brown squares and two 2½" tan 1 or cream 1 squares as shown. Sew the squares together into rows; press. Sew the rows together, carefully matching the center seams; press. Make 48 scrappy four-patch units.

Make 48.

2. Repeat step 1, substituting two 2½" blue squares for the 2½" brown squares; press. Make 12 scrappy four-patch units.

Make 12.

3. Fold each 3¾" red half-square triangle in half along the long diagonal edge to find the center point; gently finger-press to make a crease. Match the crease to the center of one edge of a four-patch unit from step 2 as shown; pin and stitch. Press the seams toward the triangle. Sew matching 3¾" red half-square triangles to the remaining sides of the unit; press. Trim the unit to 6" x 6". Make 12.

 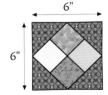

Make 12.

4. Repeat the process from step 3 to sew matching brown half-square triangles to all sides of each unit from step 3 as shown; press. Trim the unit to 8½" x 8½". Make 12.

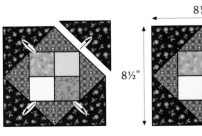

Make 12.

5. With right sides together, sew a 4⅞" red half-square triangle to the short edge of a brown quarter-square triangle as shown; press. Sew a matching 4⅞" red half-square triangle to the adjacent short edge of the brown triangle to complete a flying-geese unit. Make 48 flying-geese units in matching sets of four.

Make 48.

6. Referring to the block assembly diagram below, arrange four units from step 1, one unit from step 4, and four matching units from step 5 as shown. Sew the units together into rows; press. Sew the rows together to complete the block; press. Make 12 blocks. Each block should measure 16½" x 16½", including seam allowances.

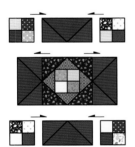

Make 12.

Make the Small Star Blocks

1. Arrange two 1½" blue squares and two 1½" tan 1 or cream 1 squares as shown. Sew the squares together into rows; press. Sew the rows together, carefully matching the center seams; press. Make 14 scrappy four-patch units.

Make 14.

2. Sew a 1½" x 2½" matching brown rectangle to opposite sides of each unit from step 1; press. Sew a 1½" x 4½" matching brown rectangle to the top and bottom; press. Make 14.

Make 14.

3. With right sides together, sew a 2⅞" red half-square triangle to the short edge of a tan 2 quarter-square triangle as shown; press. Sew a matching 2⅞" red half-square triangle to the adjacent short edge of the tan 2 triangle to complete a flying-geese unit. Make 28 flying-geese units in matching pairs.

Make 28.

4. Repeat step 3, substituting cream 2 quarter-square triangles for the tan 2 quarter-square triangles. Make 28 flying-geese units in matching pairs.

Make 28.

5. Referring to the block assembly diagram on page 60, arrange one unit from step 2, two matching units from step 3, two units with matching red triangles from step 4, and four 2½" tan 2 squares as shown. Sew the units into rows, press. Sew the rows together to complete the block; press.

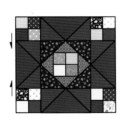

Make 10 blocks and label them Small Star block 1. Each block should measure 8½" x 8½", including seam allowances.

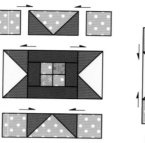

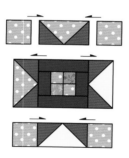

Small Star block 1.
Make 10.

6. Repeat step 5, arranging the units as shown in the block assembly diagram below. Make four blocks and label them Small Star block 2.

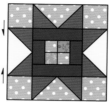

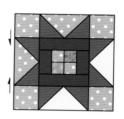

Small Star block 2.
Make 4.

Assemble the Quilt

1. Arrange and sew three Large Star blocks and two 2½" x 16½" dark brown strips, alternating them as shown to make a row; press. Make four rows.

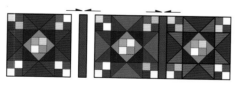

Make 4 rows.

2. Arrange and sew three 2½" x 16½" dark brown strips and two 2½" tan 1 or cream 1 squares, alternating them as shown to make a row; press. Make three rows.

Make 3 rows.

3. Referring to the quilt assembly diagram below, arrange the rows from steps 1 and 2, alternating them as shown. Sew the rows together to complete the quilt center; press.

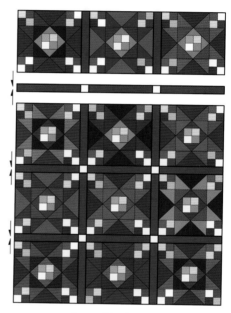

Assembly diagram

Make and Add the Outer Border

1. With right sides together, arrange and sew two 2½" x 42" tan 2 strips and one 4½" x 42" cream 2 strip together along their long edges to make a strip set as shown; press. Make five strip sets.

Make 5 strip sets.

2. Crosscut the strip sets into eight segments, 13½" wide; label them segment 1. From the remaining strip sets, crosscut six segments, 10½" wide; label them segment 2.

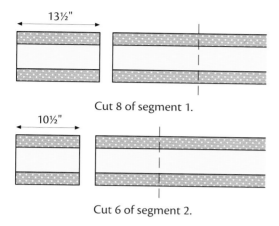

Cut 8 of segment 1.

Cut 6 of segment 2.

3. Arrange three of Small Star block 1 and two each of segments 1 and 2 as shown. Sew the blocks and segments together to make a side border; press. Make a second side border unit, rotating the stars as shown in the quilt plan.

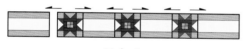

Make 2.

4. Arrange two each of Small Star block 1 and 2, two of segment 1, and one of segment 2 as shown. Sew the blocks and segments together to make the top border; press. Make a second border unit for the bottom border, rotating the stars as shown in the quilt plan.

Make 2.

5. Referring to the photo on page 56, sew the border units from step 3 to the sides of the quilt. Press the seams toward the borders. Sew the border units from step 4 to the top and bottom of the quilt; press.

Finish the Quilt

For detailed instructions on the following steps, refer to "Finishing Techniques" on page 17.

1. Cut and piece the backing fabric so that it measures 10" larger than both the length and width of the quilt top.

2. Layer the quilt top, batting, and backing together; baste.

3. Machine or hand quilt as desired.

4. Use the 2½"-wide strips to prepare the binding, and sew the binding to the quilt.

Quilt plan

lemon twist

Anyone who knows me knows I absolutely *love* lemons in just about every shape and size, so—of course—a lemon-inspired quilt was a sure bet for this book! Cheery lemon yellow and crisp white prints make for a playful combination in this quick and easy pieced and appliquéd quilt.

FINISHED QUILT: 42½" x 50½"
FINISHED BLOCK: 8" x 8"

Materials

All yardages are based on 42"-wide fabric.

- 1⅓ yards *total* of assorted white-on-white prints for blocks
- 1⅛ yards *total* of assorted yellow prints for Pinwheel and Four Patch blocks, lemon appliqués, and outer border
- 1 yard *total* of assorted green prints for Pinwheel blocks, leaf appliqués, and outer border
- ⅓ yard of green-and-white gingham check for inner border
- 10" x 10" square of yellow wool felt for large flower appliqués
- 10" x 10" square of cream wool felt for small flower appliqués
- ½ yard of fabric for binding
- 3 yards of fabric for backing (horizontal seam)
- 52" x 60" piece of batting
- ⅞ yard of 18"-wide fusible web
- Water-soluble glue
- Thread in coordinating colors for appliqué
- Brown embroidery floss (6-strand)

Cut the Fabric

Measurements include ¼" seam allowance. Cut all strips on the crosswise grain of the fabric (selvage to selvage).

From the assorted white-on-white prints, cut *a total of*:

- 10 squares, 5¼" x 5¼"; cut each square in half twice diagonally to make 40 quarter-square triangles
- 10 squares, 9½" x 9½"
- 8 squares, 2½" x 2½"

From the assorted green prints, cut *a total of*:

- 10 squares, 5¼" x 5¼"; cut each square in half twice diagonally to make 40 quarter-square triangles
- 72 rectangles, 1½" x 4½"

From the assorted yellow prints, cut *a total of*:

- 20 squares, 4⅞" x 4⅞"; cut each square in half diagonally to make 40 half-square triangles
- 8 squares, 2½" x 2½"
- 36 rectangles, 2½" x 4½"

From the green-and-white gingham check, cut:

- 2 strips, 1½" x 32½"
- 4 strips, 1½" x 4½"
- 3 strips, 1½" x 42"

From the binding fabric, cut:

- 5 strips, 2½" x 42"

Make the Pinwheel Blocks

1. With right sides together, sew a white quarter-square triangle and a green quarter-square triangle together along their short edges as shown; press. Make 40 scrappy units.

Make 40.

2. With right sides together, sew each unit from step 1 together with a yellow half-square triangle as shown; press. Make 40 scrappy units.

Make 40.

3. Referring to the block assembly diagram below, arrange four units from step 2, rotating them as shown. Sew the units together into rows; press. Sew the rows together to complete the block. Make 10 blocks. Each block should measure 8½" x 8½", including seam allowances.

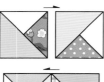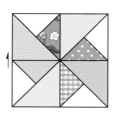

Make 10.

Make the Lemon Blocks

1. Before beginning, refer to the "Test First!" tip box on page 16. Referring to "Machine Appliqué" on page 15, use the patterns on page 67 to prepare 10 lemon appliqués (A) using the assorted yellow prints, and 10 large leaf appliqués (B) and 10 small leaf appliqués (C) using the assorted green prints. Referring to "Working with Wool-Felt Appliqué" on page 16, use the patterns on page 67 to prepare 10 large flower appliqués (D) using the yellow wool felt, and 20 small flower appliqués (E) using the cream wool felt.

2. Referring to the appliqué placement diagram below, position and fuse one lemon appliqué (A), one large leaf appliqué (B), and one small leaf appliqué (C) on each 9½" white square; allow the pieces to cool. Use coordinating thread to machine blanket stitch around the edges of each lemon and leaf. Use a small amount of water-soluble glue to tack one large flower appliqué (D) and two small flower appliqués (E) in place on each block. Make 10 blocks.

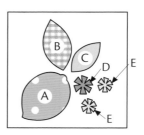

Appliqué placement diagram

3. Referring to "Hand-Embroidery Stitches" on page 16, use three strands of brown embroidery floss to make three French knots in the center of each large and small flower.

4. Trim each Lemon block to measure 8½" x 8½".

Assemble the Quilt

Referring to the quilt assembly diagram below, arrange the Pinwheel and Lemon blocks in five horizontal rows of four blocks each, alternating the blocks as shown. Press the seams in opposite directions from row to row. Sew the rows together; press.

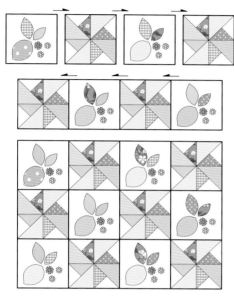

Assembly diagram

Make and Add the Borders

1. Arrange two 2½" yellow squares and two 2½" white squares as shown. Sew the squares together into rows; press. Sew the rows together, carefully matching the center seams; press. Make four Four Patch blocks.

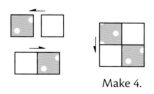

Make 4.

2. Arrange and sew sixteen 1½" x 4½" assorted green rectangles and eight 2½" x 4½" assorted yellow rectangles together along their long edges as shown. Make two outer-border strips. Sew a 1½" x 32½" gingham inner-border strip to one edge of each border strip; press. Referring to the quilt photo on page 62, sew the border units to the top and bottom of the quilt. Press the seams toward the border unit.

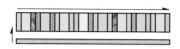

Make 2.

3. Arrange and sew two 1½" x 4½" gingham rectangles, ten 2½" x 4½" assorted yellow rectangles, and twenty 1½" x 4½" assorted green rectangles together along their long edges as shown. Sew a Four Patch block from step 1 to each end of each border; press. Make two.

4. Sew the 1½" x 42" gingham strips together end to end to make one continuous strip. From this strip, cut two 1½" x 52½" strips and sew one to each border strip from step 3; press. Sew the border units to the sides of the quilt; press.

Make 2.

Finish the Quilt

For detailed instructions on the following steps, refer to "Finishing Techniques" on page 17.

1. Cut and piece the backing fabric so that it measures 10" larger than both the length and width of the quilt top.

2. Layer the quilt top, batting, and backing together; baste.

3. Machine or hand quilt as desired.

4. Use the 2½"-wide strips to prepare the binding, and sew the binding to the quilt.

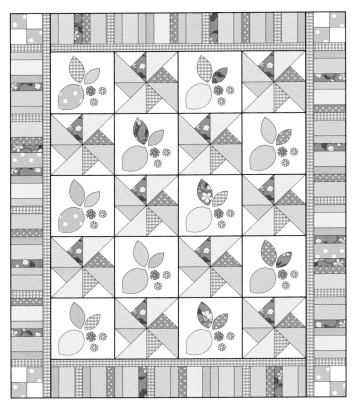

Quilt plan

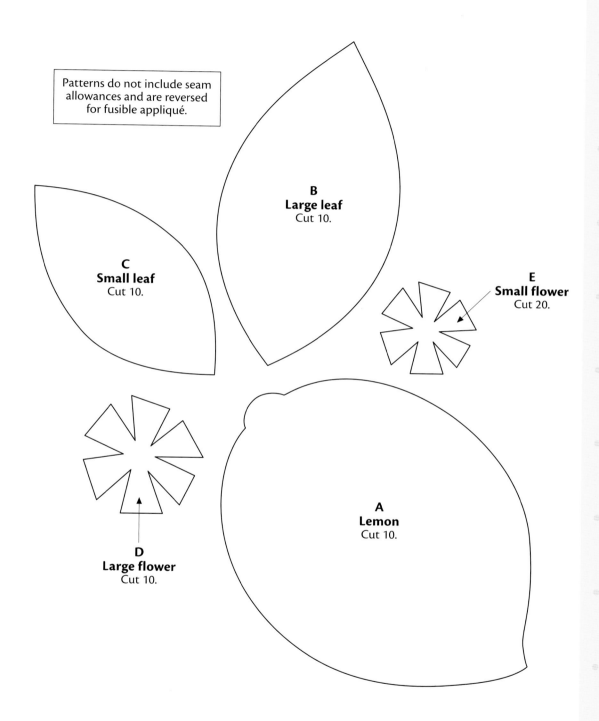

Patterns do not include seam allowances and are reversed for fusible appliqué.

B
Large leaf
Cut 10.

C
Small leaf
Cut 10.

E
Small flower
Cut 20.

D
Large flower
Cut 10.

A
Lemon
Cut 10.

ring around the posy

Join in the fun as a favorite childhood rhyme meets the quilting "playground" in this fresh take on a traditional block. Bring together cheerful prints in pink and green to create your own modern version of the traditional Courthouse Steps quilt.

Finished Quilt: 66½" x 66½"
Finished Block: 12" x 12"

Materials

Yardages are based on 42"-wide fabric.

- 1½ yards of green floral print for blocks, border corner squares, and sashing
- 1⅛ yards of pink-and-white toile for Log Cabin blocks
- 1 yard *total* of assorted white floral and light pink prints for border blocks
- ¾ yard of pink floral print for Log Cabin blocks
- ⅔ yard of red polka-dot print for blocks, sashing corner squares, inner border, and border corner squares
- ½ yard of red tone-on-tone floral print for border blocks
- ½ yard *total* of assorted light green prints for border blocks*
- ⅝ yard of fabric for binding
- 4¼ yards of fabric for backing
- 76" x 76" piece of batting

May include scraps of the green floral print.

Cut the Fabric

Measurements include ¼" seam allowance. Cut all strips on the crosswise grain of the fabric (selvage to selvage).

From the green floral print, cut:
- 19 strips, 2½" x 42"; crosscut into:
  - 26 squares, 2½" x 2½"
  - 26 rectangles, 2½" x 6½"
  - 24 strips, 2½" x 14½"

From the red polka-dot print, cut:
- 2 strips, 2½" x 42"; crosscut into 29 squares, 2½" x 2½"
- 6 strips, 2½" x 42"

From the pink floral print, cut:
- 9 strips, 2½" x 42"; crosscut into:
  - 18 rectangles, 2½" x 6½"
  - 18 rectangles, 2½" x 10½"

From the pink-and-white toile, cut:
- 14 strips, 2½" x 42"; crosscut into:
  - 18 rectangles, 2½" x 10½"
  - 18 rectangles, 2½" x 14½"

From the red tone-on-tone floral print, cut:
- 2 strips, 7¼" x 42"; crosscut into 9 squares, 7¼" x 7¼". Cut each square in half twice diagonally to make 36 quarter-square triangles.

From the assorted light green prints, cut *a total of:*

- 9 squares, 7¼" x 7¼"; cut each square in half twice diagonally to make 36 quarter-square triangles

From the assorted white floral and light pink prints, cut *a total of:*

- 18 squares, 7¼" x 7¼"; cut each square in half twice diagonally to make 72 quarter-square triangles

From the binding fabric, cut:

- 7 strips, 2½" x 42"

Make the Log Cabin Blocks

1. Sew a 2½" green floral square to opposite edges of a 2½" red polka-dot square as shown; press. Sew a 2½" x 6½" green floral rectangle to the top and bottom edges; press. Make 13. Set four units aside for the outer border.

Make 13.

2. Sew a 2½" x 6½" pink floral rectangle to opposite sides of a unit from step 1 as shown; press. Sew a 2½" x 10½" pink floral rectangle to the top and bottom edges; press. Make nine.

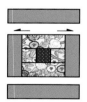

Make 9.

3. Sew a 2½" x 10½" toile rectangle to opposite sides of each unit from step 2 as shown; press. Sew a 2½" x 14½" toile rectangle to the top and bottom edges to complete the block; press. Make nine blocks. Each block should measure 14½" x 14½", including seam allowances.

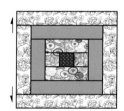 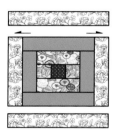

Make 9.

Assemble the Quilt

1. Arrange and sew three Log Cabin blocks and four 2½" x 14½" green floral strips, alternating them as shown to make a row; press. Make three rows.

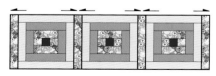

Make 3 rows.

2. Arrange and sew three 2½" x 14½" green floral strips and four 2½" red polka-dot squares, alternating them as shown to make a row; press. Make four rows.

Make 4 rows.

3. Referring to the quilt assembly diagram below, arrange the rows from steps 1 and 2, alternating them as shown. Sew the rows together to complete the quilt center. Press the seams toward the rows of sashing and corner squares.

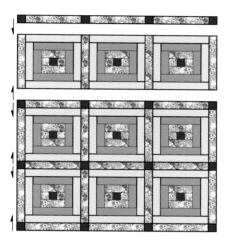

Assembly diagram

4. Sew the 2½" x 42" red polka-dot strips together end to end to make one continuous strip. From this strip, cut two 2½" x 50½" inner-border strips and sew them to the sides of the quilt. Press the seams toward the border.

5. From the remaining strip, cut two 2½" x 54½" inner-border strips, and sew them to the top and bottom of the quilt; press.

Make and Add the Outer Border

1. Arrange one red tone-on-tone quarter-square triangle, one assorted light green quarter-square triangle, and two assorted white and/or pink quarter-square triangles as shown. With right sides together, sew the triangles together in pairs along their short edges; press. Sew the pairs together; press. Make 36 Hourglass blocks. Each block should measure 6½" x 6½", including seam allowances.

Make 36.

2. Arrange and sew nine Hourglass blocks from step 1 together to make a pieced outer-border unit as shown; press. Make four.

Make 4.

3. Referring to the photo on page 68, sew an outer-border unit from step 2 to opposite sides of the quilt. Press the seams toward the outer border. Sew a unit set aside in step 1 of "Make the Log Cabin Blocks" to each end of each remaining border unit as shown; press. Make two and sew them to the top and bottom of the quilt; press.

Make 2.

Finish the Quilt

For detailed instructions on the following steps, refer to "Finishing Techniques" on page 17.

1. Cut and piece the backing fabric so that it measures 10" larger than both the length and width of the quilt top.

2. Layer the quilt top, batting, and backing together; baste.

3. Machine or hand quilt as desired.

4. Use the 2½"-wide strips to prepare the binding, and sew the binding to the quilt.

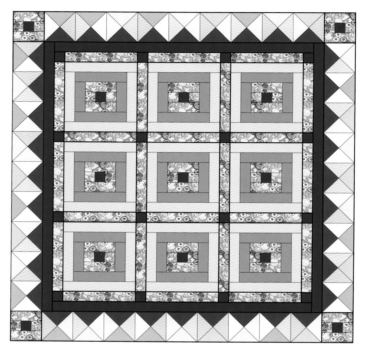

Quilt plan

ladybug jamboree

Ladybugs dance the night away in this delightful quilt featuring both large and small pieced Ladybug blocks. Appliquéd and embroidered features add personality and flair—try adding your choice of unique embellishments to this quilt to make it truly your own.

FINISHED QUILT: 40½" x 40½"
FINISHED BLOCK: 15" x 15"

Materials

Yardages are based on 42"-wide fabric. Fat quarters measure 18" x 22".

- ¾ yard *total* of assorted black prints for blocks, and antennae and ladybug spot appliqués
- ¾ yard *total* of assorted yellow prints for Ladybug 2 blocks and outer border
- ⅔ yard *total* of assorted green prints for Ladybug 2 blocks and outer border*
- ½ yard of medium tone-on-tone green print for inner border
- ½ yard *total* of assorted red prints for Ladybug 2 blocks
- Fat quarter *each* of 2 red prints for Ladybug 1 blocks
- ½ yard of fabric for binding
- 2⅞ yards of fabric for backing
- 50" x 50" piece of batting
- ¾ yard of 18"-wide fusible web
- Black embroidery floss (6-strand)

*May include scraps of the medium green tone-on-tone inner-border print.

Cut the Fabric

Measurements include ¼" seam allowance. Cut all strips on the crosswise grain of the fabric (selvage to selvage).

From *each* fat quarter of red print, cut:

- 1 square, 15⅞" x 15⅞; cut each square in half diagonally to make 2 half-square triangles (4 total)

From the assorted black prints, cut *a total of*:

- 2 squares, 8" x 8"
- 8 squares, 4⅜" x 4⅜"

From the assorted red prints, cut *a total of*:

- 8 squares, 6⅝" x 6⅝"; cut each square in half diagonally to make 16 half-square triangles

From the assorted yellow prints, cut *a total of*:

- 4 strips, 1¼" x 25"
- 16 squares, 2⅜" x 2⅜"; cut each square in half diagonally to make 32 half-square triangles
- 8 squares, 2" x 2"
- 28 squares, 3⅜" x 3⅜"; cut each square in half diagonally to make 56 half-square triangles
- 4 squares, 3" x 3"

From the assorted green prints, cut *a total of*:

- 4 strips, 1¼" x 25"
- 16 squares, 2⅜" x 2⅜"; cut each square in half diagonally to make 32 half-square triangles
- 28 squares, 3⅜" x 3⅜"; cut each square in half diagonally to make 56 half-square triangles
- 4 squares, 3" x 3"

From the medium tone-on-tone green print, cut:

- 4 strips, 3" x 30½"

From the binding fabric, cut:

- 5 strips, 2½" x 42"

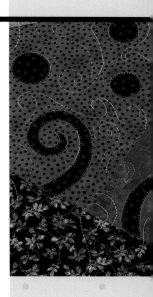

Make the Ladybug Blocks

You will make two different Ladybug blocks for this quilt: two each of Ladybug block 1 and Ladybug block 2.

LADYBUG BLOCK 1

1. With right sides together, sew one large half-square triangle of each red print together along their diagonal edges as shown; press. Make two half-square-triangle units.

 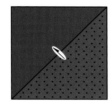

Make 2.

2. Use a ruler and your preferred marker to mark a light diagonal line on the wrong side of each 8" black square. With right sides together, align a marked square with one corner of a unit from step 1 as shown. Stitch directly on the marked line and trim, leaving a ¼" seam allowance; press. Each block should measure 15½" x 15½", including seam allowances.

Make 2.

3. Referring to "Machine Appliqué" on pages 15, use the patterns on page 79 to prepare two regular and two reversed antenna appliqués (A), four large spot appliqués (B), and eight small spot appliqués (C) using the assorted black prints.

4. Referring to the appliqué placement diagram below, position and fuse one regular and one reversed antenna appliqué (A), two large spot appliqués (B), and four small spot appliqués on each block; allow the appliqués to cool. Use coordinating thread to machine blanket stitch around the edges of each antenna and spot. Make two blocks.

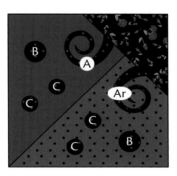

Appliqué placement diagram

LADYBUG BLOCK 2

1. Referring to "Ladybug Block 1," steps 1 and 2, make a total of eight small ladybug units using the small assorted red half-square triangles and the 4⅜" assorted black squares.

Make 8.

2. Arrange four units from step 1, rotating them as shown. Sew the units together into rows; press. Sew the rows together; press. Make two.

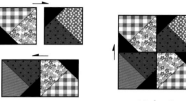

Make 2.

3. Referring to the block assembly diagram on page 77, use your preferred marker to lightly mark two antennae onto each ladybug unit in each block from step 2. Referring to "Hand-Embroidery Stitches" on page 16, use three strands of black embroidery floss and a stem stitch to embroider the antennae onto each block.

4. Sew the four 1¼" x 25" yellow strips and the four 1¼" x 25" green print strips together along their long edges, alternating them to make a scrappy strip set as shown. Crosscut the strip set into 16 segments, 1¼" wide.

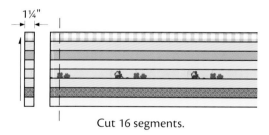

Cut 16 segments.

5. Sew two segments from step 4 together, rotating one segment as shown; press. Make eight checkerboard units. Each unit should measure 2" x 6½", including seam allowances.

Make 8.

6. With right sides together, sew one 2⅜" yellow half-square triangle and one 2⅜" green half-square triangle together along their diagonal edges as shown; press. Make 32 scrappy half-square-triangle units.

Make 32.

7. Join four scrappy half-square-triangle units from step 6 as shown; press. Make four of each.

Make 4 of each.

8. Sew one unit from step 5 and one unit from step 7 together as shown; press. Make four of each.

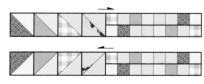

Make 4 of each.

9. Referring to the block assembly diagram below, arrange one unit from step 3, two of each unit from step 8, and four 2" assorted yellow squares. Sew the units and squares together into rows; press. Sew the rows together to complete the block; press. Make two blocks. Each block should measure 15½" x 15½", including seam allowances.

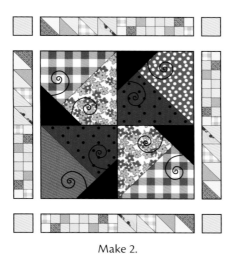

Make 2.

Assemble the Quilt

1. Referring to the quilt assembly diagram below, arrange the Ladybug 1 and Ladybug 2 blocks into two rows of two blocks each as shown. Sew the blocks together into rows. Press the seams in opposite directions for each row. Sew the rows together to complete the quilt center; press.

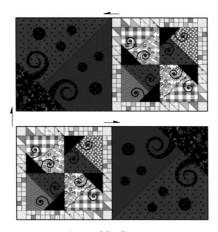

Assembly diagram

2. Sew a 3" x 30½" medium green inner-border strip to opposite sides of the quilt. Press the seams toward the border. Sew a 3" green print square to each end of each remaining inner-border strip; press. Make two and sew them to the top and bottom of the quilt center; press.

Make 2.

3. With right sides together, sew one 3⅜" yellow half-square triangle and one 3⅜" green print half-square triangle together along their diagonal edges as shown; press. Make 56 scrappy half-square-triangle units.

Make 56.

4. Sew 14 half-square-triangle units from step 3 together, turning them at the mid-point as shown; press. Make four.

Make 4.

5. Referring to the photo on page 73, sew two outer-border units from step 4 to opposite sides of the quilt. Press the seams toward the outer-border units. Sew a 3" yellow square to each end of each remaining outer-border unit; press. Make two and sew them to the top and bottom of the quilt; press.

Finish the Quilt

For detailed instructions on the following steps, refer to "Finishing Techniques" on page 17.

1. Cut and piece the backing fabric so that it measures 10" larger than both the length and width of the quilt top.

2. Layer the quilt top, batting, and backing together; baste.

3. Machine or hand quilt as desired.

4. Use the 2½"-wide strips to prepare the binding, and sew the binding to the quilt.

Quilt plan

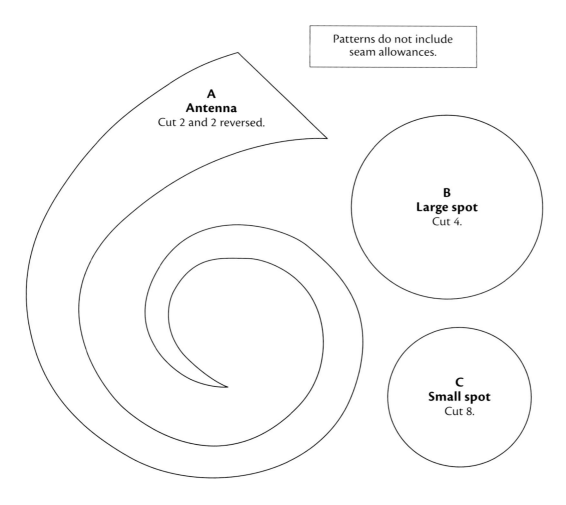

Patterns do not include seam allowances.

A
Antenna
Cut 2 and 2 reversed.

B
Large spot
Cut 4.

C
Small spot
Cut 8.

about the author

Cyndi Walker was born in California and received a degree in fashion art and advertising from Virginia Commonwealth University. As a graphic designer and illustrator, she has always been active in the creative arts, and eventually found an outlet for her talents in quilting. From her very first quilting class, she was hooked, and she currently enjoys teaching at local quilt shops, hunting for new and exciting fabrics, and designing quilts for her pattern company, Stitch Studios. Known for their playful colors and sense of whimsy, her designs reflect the idea that quilting should always be fun!

Cyndi lives with her family and two dogs in the Seattle, Washington, area.